Top Dog

This is Top Dog.

I can flip.
Flip!
I can kick.
Kick!
Spin!
I can spin things.

This is the Bad Dog Bunch.

My job is to stop the Bad Dog Bunch robbing shops.

The Bad Dog Bunch rob the pet shop.

They hop into the van and dash off.

Top Dog has a plan.

Top Dog stops the van!

The Bad Dog Bunch get a shock!

They can not go on!

Top Dog is a champ!